PREACHING FORWARD

Calling
Character
Craft

SAMUEL DEUTH

CONTENTS

SAMUELDEUTH.COM
PREACHINGFORWARD.COM

SECTION ONE
THE RESPONSE

CHAPTER 1

PREACHERS:
THE RESPONSE OF HEAVEN

*Then I heard the voice of the Lord saying, "Whom shall I send? And who
will go for us?" And I said, "Here am I. Send me!"*
— *Isaiah 6:8 (NIV)*

You are the response of Heaven to the cry of your
generation! As a preacher and conduit of the message of
the Gospel, you're not just an extra you're a necessity to the
purpose that God is working out here on Earth! While
you're a flawed instrument, you are His chosen vessel to
communicate His most important message to the people
He so desperately loves.

The declaring of the Gospel brings freedom, healing,
and reconciliation to its hearers, which is why the enemy
works to silence the voice of the leaders of God's people.
As you walk in your calling to preach and teach the Word
of God, you will have to push past the things that would
leave your message powerless or ineffective.

The nation and city you've been placed in is strategic,
but that doesn't mean that it will be easy or automatic. God
is looking for men and women with boldness who will be

willing to say, "Here am I. Send me!" Preachers who won't back down or back up from proclaiming the word of God! It's the only hope our world has.

This book is more than an instructional book on how to write a sermon and preach; it's a call to give yourself fully to Jesus and the message He's commissioned you to deliver! Don't think small of yourself or lightly about the call you've received.

You're not here on this planet, in this era by chance, but by God's appointment!

SUCH A TIME AS THIS!

In the book of Esther, we see this play out between God's people and a young Jewish girl named Esther. This story parallels the world we live in today: The enemy had devised a plan to destroy God's people and purpose, and we also see God's consistent work at play as the cry of the people reached Heaven. God then orchestrates a plan to have a young woman perfectly positioned to shift the outcome of the plan of the enemy and rescue a generation.

I encourage you to read the whole book of Esther again with this context in mind, but what I'll focus on is the epic conversation that saves a generation. The plot to kill all of the Jews reaches the ears of Esther's cousin and informant, Mordecai. He calls on her to step in and speak to the King. This seems logical, but in that context she explains that she could be killed. When she sends that message back to Mordecai, he sends back a powerful challenge and insight into the key need for preachers in this era as well:

For if you remain silent at this time, relief and deliverance for the Jews will arise from another place, but you and your father's family will perish. And who knows but that you have come to your royal position for such a time as this?"
— *Esther 4:14 (NIV)*

He says if you remain "silent at this time" it will result in the destruction of this generation. But you may be thinking, "didn't God say He would bring deliverance from someone else?" True, and ultimately God will work His purpose on the Earth no matter our obedience or disobedience, but that doesn't mean there aren't negative implications to our disobedience. If God has called you to preach and you remain silent, God will raise up other preachers, but there will be people that you were specifically positioned for "such a time as this" to impact who may never hear the Gospel as a result.

You and I cannot afford to assume that our obedience to the call of God impacts only me and my life, when, in reality, if He's placed you in this time and called you to be His messenger, then you better believe that your voice is not only valuable but necessary!

When the church loses its voice,
the world loses its way.
– Leanne Matthesius

THE CALL CONTINUES
TO GO OUT!

This generational positioning by the Holy Spirit to have the right voice, in the right place, at the right time, isn't just something that happened in Biblical times with people like Noah, David, Samson, Esther, Moses, Joshua, Peter, Paul, Abigail, Joseph, John the Baptist and so many more. It's still something that God is doing to this very day.

Like Kevin Gerald often says, "The Church is plan A, there is no plan B." In saying this he was reinforcing the reality that God has placed the privilege of and responsibility of advancing the Gospel on the shoulders of the church and He doesn't have a backup plan. That's why He sent us His Spirit to empower us for the work. And just like the broader collective of believers is responsible to carry the message of Jesus, we as preachers are the front runners of leading the way in declaring truth and raising up others to do the same. Preachers aren't the only ones bringing good news, in fact, a key part of our role is to raise up the broader church to carry the message to every corner of the Earth!

So, I firmly believe that if you're hearing the call of God to preach and teach His Word, then you'll want embrace that call with appreciation for the privilege and soberness of the eternal impact of your response. Eternity is literally in the balance for countless multitudes that will be impacted over the generations as a result of people encountering the truth of God's Word through you.

THE WORLD IS IN DESPERATE NEED OF PREACHERS

In a world of confusion and uncertainty, we need men and women who declare the word of God with boldness and clarity, because only in this declaration of truth is there any hope! Many of societies struggles and hardships are a result of lack of truth or the messaging that there is a plurality of truths. We can compromise on preferences and opinions, but where the Word of God is clear, we must be also. As a rule, speak where God speaks, and be silent where He's silent. Which means don't feel the need fill in gaps that Jesus never did. For years we got caught in this trap of making rules where God didn't; this is when we slip into religion, following the way of the pharisees of Jesus era.

When he saw the crowds, he had compassion on them, because they were harassed and helpless, like sheep without a shepherd.
— Matthew 9:36 (NIV)

When we look out into the city that God has placed us in, we need to see what Jesus sees, people without guidance or revelation. People who are wandering aimlessly and need someone with courage to call them back to the only thing that will give peace and fulfillment to their lives—Jesus.

Preachers are guides for people. It's so important that we understand this function, because we're not just here to say nice things that people want to hear and dance around difficult issues, we're called to guide people through life's dark valleys and confusion back to the clarity of God's Word.

Preachers aren't performers; we're on a mission.

We're laboring with Christ to mature, strengthen and lead His people forward. You're not preaching to "not offend," you're preaching to advance their lives; which is the reason why I titled this book *Preaching Forward.* Our preaching should equip and inspire people towards Jesus and His purpose for their lives!

PREACHERS REVEAL
GOD'S HEART

As preachers, one of the key roles we've been given is to echo Heaven. How you view God and think about Him matters. Who is He to you? Is God a task master? An angry dictator? A distant creator? or is He a loving father, savior, and friend. As I've had the privilege of being a father to my two beautiful girls, Mercedes and Kenzie, God has used that to give me glimpses and windows into the level of how much God truly loves us. We are the local representative of the heart of God. When I remind myself of that truth it impacts what I say, and how I say it. If I remember that I'm a steward and an ambassador of Heaven, then I bring His message to His people to advance His kingdom.

So, while we do want to be open and authentic as preachers, ultimately what I'm trying to reveal is not my heart but the heart and nature of God. All of my authenticity is not to draw people to me but to reveal more of the heart of God as it encounters my humanity.

WHO WILL GO?

Why do we even have preachers? The answer to that is pretty simple; because God has a message!

Then I heard the voice of the Lord saying, "Whom shall I send? And who will go for us?" And I said, "Here am I. Send me!"
— Isaiah 6:8 (NIV)

As long as there's still a message that God is needing to communicate to people there will always be a demand for a preacher or a voice to bring that message to people! It's a powerful look into the process of the calling of a preacher. The call goes out, the request comes to Earth, and God is looking for a willing vessel and messenger for His Gospel message!

Sometimes we may not have been the first choice, but just the preacher who said yes! I remember hearing the story that Kathryn Kuhlman shares about God keeping her walking in humility by reminding her that she was well down the list of choices for the ministry that she ultimately built, but that she was just the one to finally say, "Yes, Send Me!"

CHAPTER 2

PREACHERS BRING GOOD NEWS!

What is our message as preachers? It's all built upon the message of the Gospel. The Gospel means "Good News". It's important that we remember this; our message is good! We literally have the best news! When we get off centered from this reality we start assuming we're the enforcers sent to rough anyone up that slips up along the way. I've heard countless testimonies over the years of people encountering bad news from preachers rather than good news. Do people feel infused with the hope that comes from the good news or do they feel weighed down by the hopelessness of their sin?

For God so loved the world that he gave his one and only Son, that whoever believes in him shall not perish but have eternal life. For God did not send his Son into the world to condemn the world, but to save the world through him.
— John 3:16-17 (NIV)

I mean, wow! The creator of all of the universe left Heaven to rescue us in our sin and brokenness! And, when he came, instead of coming with judgement, He came with Grace and Salvation!

When I was younger, I'd say I would say I fell more into a harsher stance as a Christian. More legalistic and ready to quickly condemn people in their sin, Christians and Non-Christians. But I'm thankful for grace, time, maturity and my own failures that have caused me to wake up to the goodness of God and his grace towards not only the "whole world," but, more specifically, that this Good News became personally available to me.

As I've grown as a preacher I'm reminded how much we need to be leading with the Good News! If our messages are leaning more towards being harsh and heavy handed versus full of grace and love, then we're doing something wrong.

One of the greatest displays of this was when Jesus was confronted with the women caught in adultery. He perfectly displayed why and how He came and how to apply the Gospel. When everyone else was pointing out her sin, Jesus pointed to the Good News: that He didn't come here to condemn us, but to forgive and set us free to live!

Are our messages the healing salve that the good Samaritan put on the broken and beat up traveler? Or do our messages put us at arm's length from the point of the pain that people are dealing with? Let's build our preaching with the foundational desire to help people see that all of the barriers have been eliminated between us and God and through the cross we're invited to come near!

But now in Christ Jesus you who once were far away have been brought near by the blood of Christ.
— Ephesians 2:13 (NIV)

PREACHERS BRING
HEAVEN TO EARTH

Collectively as preachers, we are moving the purposes of God forward; we're helping the church establish the Kingdom of Heaven on Earth. We're bringing to fulfilment the prayer Jesus taught us to pray, "Your Kingdom come on Earth as it is in Heaven." This isn't just a nice prayer for ceremonies and formal gatherings, this is the heart and goal that we have to keep in mind. We're on a mission and we have marching orders and it's our role as the church to continue to take ground for the Kingdom of Heaven here on Earth. That's why He calls on us to preach and lead with boldness and resolve. Don't give up ground to the enemy!

In a home, the thermostat is what sets the temperature, and God has positioned us as preachers to be thermostats in the culture and church. The challenge is that too many of us as preacher have settled for being a thermometer. We're writing messages only based off taking a reading of the current temperature rather than using God's Word to set a new temperature. In each church gathering, we have an opportunity to re-set the room to the temperature of truth. Our world we live in can tend to cool us off, so don't meet people in their lukewarm level, call them up and inject faith into their worlds!

PREACHERS INJECT
GRACE & TRUTH

This is an important conversation to have in light of the depravity in culture and the religiosity of our churches.

I know that's a big statement, especially the second half, but it's true. We need to not let up on dispensing both grace and truth in our messages. And don't worry about going overboard in either direction, just preach with 100% of both. Notice how it says Jesus came:

The Word became flesh and made his dwelling among us. We have seen his glory, the glory of the one and only Son, who came from the Father, full of grace and truth.
— John 1:14 (NIV)

Jesus came full of Grace & Truth! It doesn't say He was 50% truth and 50% grace, He was fully and completely both. We don't have to withhold grace to bring truth and we don't have to soften the truth to have grace.

I remember a time when my wife and I were ministering at the LA Dream Center with Matthew Barnett, and I was wrestling with this thought of how much truth do you bring to the homeless and broken people on the streets of LA versus how much mercy and grace do you show. And in the core of me, I had this wrong thinking in me that felt like we needed to be measured in our grace and mercy until they proved worthy of it. Sounds horrible to write out, but it's the reality. I remember asking Matthew if it's good to give food to the same people over and over if there's no change, and his response slapped me in the face and called me to live a life of greater no-strings-attached love. He looked at me like I was asking the dumbest question in the world! Ha! He just simply said, "No, we keep showing compassion because that next meal could open the door to share hope and the gospel with them."

Our world is desperate and starving for both grace and truth. They need to know they're loved before they perform well or regardless of their performance, and that there is The Way and The Truth, because only in the truth can they find freedom. Don't withhold an ounce of either.

My personality leans towards just wanting everyone to like me all the time. I mean, I'm a nice person!! Ha! And because of that in my early years of ministry leadership it would cause me to withhold the truth because I didn't want to hurt or offend someone. But, over the years what I learned was that if I really loved people the way I say I do, then I'll bring them the full truth. So, now I love having difficult conversations because I know how much it will help people. In the same way, when I preach, I don't have an issue bringing a truth from God's Word that people might not want to hear, because I know that it will set them free.

.

THE GOOD NEWS HOLDS POWER!

One of the key elements of the Good News is that it's not empty words, but it's full of power! The Good News about Jesus isn't just well wishes and good vibes, it isn't just principles and good behavioral advice, the Word of God carries His power! The Word of God carries within it power and authority.

If you're preaching the Word of God and not expecting a flow of power, then you're massively underutilizing your gift and calling as a preacher. The Holy Spirit is available to the believer and partners with His word to fulfill it!

Then the disciples went out and preached everywhere, and the Lord worked with them and confirmed his word by the signs that accompanied it.
— Mark 16:20 (NIV)

We'll talk more about preaching with authority and power, but initially I'll note that many church leaders have backed away from expecting God's power to partner with their preaching. I fell into this category for many years. While I knew that God could heal and deliver, I never actually engaged the power of God's Word in its fullest extent. When we preach, but don't expect God to heal, deliver or save during the preaching and teaching, we reduced the Gospel to a bedtime story.

CHAPTER 3

PREACHERS SHOW GOD'S WAY

We are not Christian entertainers; we have a purpose and focus as we preach. We're here to equip and mature God's people. This is an essential perspective that shapes how we develop the message and how we engage with our audience. In the great commission we're commanded by Jesus to teach them to obey everything, this means that we're not just giving nice studies, we're focused and intentional with our messages to form and shape and develop people.

USE YOUR VOICE

One of the things I need to lean into in this section is the need for preachers to fully embrace, not only the privilege to shape God's people, but the responsibility to do so.

If we're not careful we'll lean into this call when we know people will like what we're saying and then shy away from the message when we know what we're about to say could ruffle some feathers or get people uncomfortable. Our responsibility to train, teach and instruct people in the way that Jesus taught us, continues regardless of social and public opinion.

As a parent, there are many things I have to say to my kids that I know they won't want to hear, but my wife Katie and I say it anyway because we love our kids and truly want the best for them. As preachers and communicators of God's truth, sometimes there are going to be things that we know people will not want to hear, or we may have to point people away from something in culture and back to His word. We'll have to be ready to stay committed to bringing them the essential message of God's Word no matter what!

Each of us has to make our own decision on what cultural or social issues we jump into as Christian leaders, but I want to encourage you to not withhold your voice if it has the ability to establish or advance God's will and ways in your culture. Even politically, it can depend on the nation you're in. In my nation, USA, I have the ability to positively impact the nation in the direction of God's will and ways, so I feel an obligation to engage and shift our culture. Some of you reading this might be in nations that you have no voting and democratic process, and so your approach to impacting culture will have to be a different route.

For me, I consider that iconic statement and really indictment from the book of Esther, "If you remain silent at this time," to determine whether I speak up or not within the generation that I've been placed.

And even within focused context of people's personal lives and families, if we have God's Word but withhold it, we need to remember the collateral damage that it could cause to people's present and futures. My tendency is to just want people to like me, so with God's help I learned that if I really love people then I'll bring them the truth they need to hear.

LEAD BY EXAMPLE

In this world, some of the most important messages that we'll ever preach are not on stages or with microphones but with our lives.

We often put too much emphasis on the public skill and gifting and not enough on our private world. But, we don't impart and give what we don't have inside. You can teach principles, but the full weight and impact of your preaching will only happen when what you say is matched with who you are off the stage.

First, as a follower of Jesus, I must live consistently with the message of Jesus, so that I can be a credible testimony of the message of Jesus. But even more as a preacher, I must lead the way in my life, speech, actions, money, relationships and more.

PREACHERS RELEASE
FAITH TO BELIEVE

One of the main goals I have when I preach is to leave them with more faith and courage than when I began! Having faith and believing is such a central theme of scripture, and it must remain a primary focus for us as preachers if we're going to see people's lives take ground.

Clothe your audience with faith!
— Phil Pringle | C3 Church Global

Life's circumstances tend to little by little deplete our faith and confidence, but that's where we as preachers come in to be the voice that points them back to belief! Notice how often message of faith come in scripture, like be strong, take courage, don't be afraid, trust God and many more phrases like that, all of these messages speaking the need that we as humans have to be continually encouraged. I think many see encouragement as a reward, but I'd like to challenge you to see it as a catalyst. Without faith it's impossible to please God and impossible to fulfill your purpose!

> *Jesus told him, "Don't be afraid; just believe."*
> — *Mark 5:36 (NIV)*

PREACHERS MOVE THE CHURCH FORWARD!

We are here on mission. As preachers we need to remember that we're not just doing a job and preforming a Christian duty, we're called on by God to build up and rally God's people towards a certain direction. The great commission that we've been given is not simply a story in the Bible it is the mandate that you and I must carry.

In the Kingdom of God, we're working to preach in a way that instills faith, courage and strategy into the hearts of people, so that they activate God's calling on their lives! God gave his people the promise that He'd give them everywhere that their feet stepped, but many don't experience it because they don't step in faith toward the promises of God.

Now, we don't need to accomplish the whole mission in one message. There are many messages that you'll preach over your lifetime, and most of your listeners will hear hundreds and thousands of messages, so our goal with the next message is to move things forward one more step for people.

We're also commissioned with the mandate to call people to live out the Bible in their personal lives. This means we're change agents. God wants to use your message to be a catalyst for people to make the changes they need to make. Don't settle for people just feeling good after your message, make it your goal to help them be able to take that next step of faith and obedience.

What's the biggest way to make that happen? The Power of God's Word in their lives! It's the consistent and continual application of God's Word that causes the transformation in people's lives. Like many have said, "Let's preach to their Monday!" Saying that we want to be sure that we're bringing the Word in a way that they can begin to take steps in that direction right away.

He is the one we proclaim, admonishing and teaching everyone with all wisdom, so that we may present everyone fully mature in Christ. To this end I strenuously contend with all the energy Christ so powerfully works in me.
— Colossians 1:28-29 (NIV)

CHAPTER 4

4 FOCUSES BEFORE YOU PREACH

Whether you're just discovering and stepping into your calling as a preacher or you've been preaching for decades, I find that these areas of focus are key to have as targets and guardrails to keep me effective and productive as a preacher!

JESUS CENTRAL

I know this seems obvious, but if there's a warning in the Bible to the early church about losing their first love, then it's one of those things that has to be clarified. And not only because it's in the Bible from a historical standpoint, but also, as a passionate follower of Jesus, I've had very Jesus focused seasons and I've had seasons where it feels like I'm just going through the motions. It's easy to slip into that if we're not careful.

This is why my personal devotional time with Jesus must be authentic and consistent. I don't read the Bible just to get messages, I let the Bible read me! And I use the

Following Jesus One Year Bible reading plan to keep me getting a daily and consistent intake from God's Word.

All impactful preaching is going to be an overflow of your time with Jesus. We must keep Jesus at not only the center of our preaching but, as a preacher, He must be the central focus of our own lives. Do you know and love Jesus? I'm serious; how's your relationship with him? Don't go through the motions of trying to "do" ministry when you're not in the overflow of a relationship with Jesus.

My preaching won't be effective if it's not Jesus central. If I'm not pointing people to Him, then I need to retire today. If I'm not calling people close to the presence of God, then whose message do I think I'm delivering?

His Presence

Are you making His presence your pursuit? His presence changes everything! Many Christians live dry and missing the richness of the life of faith, because there's no engagement with His presence. There's a lot of rules and "effort" and doing the "work" of ministry, but it's all push and strain and no ease. The Spirit of God and His presence are like the oil in a vehicle; without it the vehicle will end up overheating and ultimately grinding to a halt. The following two verses in Psalm 27 have been key verses over the years that have given words to my hearts pursuit to be in the presence of God!

One thing I ask from the Lord, this only do I seek: that I may dwell in the house of the Lord all the days of my life, to gaze on the beauty of the Lord and to seek him in his temple.
— Psalm 27:4 (NIV)

When You said, "Seek My face [in prayer, require My presence as your greatest need]," my heart said to You, "Your face, O Lord, I will seek [on the authority of Your word]."
— Psalm 27:8 (AMP)

His Word

Are you focused on His word? Not just studying it for the next message you're going to preach, but have you allowed the Holy Spirit to give you a deep and unquenchable passion to consume the Bible! His words are life and light to you first and then to your audience.

One of the first things I tell new people who feel called into to ministry is to fall in the love with the Word! It's the word of God that carries the power of God! Within the truth and wisdom of the Bible, we find the transforming power of God. We're transformed and renewed by the word of God. The most transforming messages have been preached by men and women who have first been transformed by the message.

As preachers we're planters of the Word of God into the hearts of people. The word is the seed that grows and expands until it fills every part of my heart and reaches to every corner of the world!

The Word of God is what liberates and transforms. The world you live in doesn't just need inspiration and motivation or some type of self-help quote and social media meme, this world desperately needs the undiluted powerful truth of God's Word!

The truth of God's Word is the only hope of this world.

His Gospel

The power to save humanity is found within the Gospel. The Gospel is the Good News about Jesus! Do you know how to tell someone the Gospel? Do you know how to simply, boldly and clearly articulate the Gospel and passionately call people to respond to it?

It's so key that we keep this as a primary focus of our lives, our churches, and our preaching. Eternity is hanging in the balance for people; we don't want someone coming to church and just getting self-help training, everyone must be lovingly called to a point of decision.

Only the Gospel holds hope for humanity.

I get the privilege to be one of the instructors in our Internship program at C3 Church, I teach the preaching intensive course and it's one of the highlights of my year! In one of my recent classes I asked everyone to articulate the gospel. If they were to talk with someone, how would they describe the most crucial message that we have. One of the things that I noticed was that they all had slightly different ways and approaches to articulating the gospel. Some of that we talked through to help bring more focus and clarity, but in a general sense, we're all going to describe the gospel in our own unique way. And that's ok, because Jesus has engaged each of us individually and in our own way. My basic way of describing the Gospel is:

God loves us and wants us to be close to Him. So even through our sin separated us from Him, He sent Jesus to break the power of the enemy, forgive our sins, and bring us close to Him again!

The Gospel is not something you can be indifferent towards; you accept it or you reject it. Make sure people get that privilege when you preach, to come into full contact with the message of the Gospel and be able to choose to put their faith in Jesus.

PEOPLE FOCUSED

This focus as a preacher cannot be overstated. In a me centered and self-promoting culture, we must resist that and maintain a focus on serving people the way Jesus set out for us. As extensions of him and of his message, we have to remember first of all that we speak to people on HIS BEHALF.

Do not speak to people how you want, but how you know that Jesus would want you to communicate. Sometimes we can be guilty of communicating a message to someone on behalf of someone else and not deliver it with the same emotions that it was delivered in. And as preacher we can end up using God's Word to beat people up and bring condemnation, rather than to speak hope and life.

Feed The Sheep

The shepherd is a common concept used to describe God, and to describe the role that we as ministry leaders play as extensions of the Great Shepherd, Jesus.

When they had finished eating, Jesus said to Simon Peter, "Simon son of John, do you love me more than these?" "Yes, Lord," He said, "you know that I love you." Jesus said, "Feed my lambs." Again Jesus said, "Simon son of John, do you love me?" He answered, "Yes, Lord, you know that I love you." Jesus said, "Take care of my sheep." The third time He said to him, "Simon son of John, do you love me?" Peter was hurt because Jesus asked him the third time, "Do you love me?" He said, "Lord, you know

all things; you know that I love you." Jesus said, "Feed my sheep. Very truly I tell you, when you were younger you dressed yourself and went where you wanted; but when you are old you will stretch out your hands, and someone else will dress you and lead you where you do not want to go." Jesus said this to indicate the kind of death by which Peter would glorify God. Then He said to him, "Follow me!"
— John 21:15-19 (NIV)

In this powerful exchange that Jesus has with Peter, we see not only that loving Jesus personally is a prerequisite to ministry; we see that our love for God should cause us to love and feed His sheep. While we have been delegated roles and spheres of responsibility, we have to keep in mind that we are serving on His behalf and are under-shepherds for Jesus.

So, this drives our messages we develop; is what you're preaching, feeding and caring for people like Jesus intends?

In one sense, just about any message we put together that's biblically accurate will have a level of "feeding" to it. But, let's also consider the spirit in which we bring the message. Just like in general interpersonal communication, it's not always what you say, but how you say it. The audience can feel how you see them, and will respond accordingly.

You can bring encouragement or you can bring correction, and both can feed and build up the church when the delivery of those messages flows from a love for God and heart to serve and love His people.

Do you love people? If that's not an easy yes, then ask God to give you a heart for the people He's called you to minister to.

Care For People

Sometimes in preaching we can get puffed up on knowledge or get almost to a place of arrogance as we deliver a hard-hitting truth that we know is about to "get them" right where they're off track.

We've missed the Father's heart when our one-liners and in-your-face quotes aren't done out of love and care for people, but out of a need to get an "attaboy" for coming up with something slick that no one in recent history has said. A father who cares about his kids would never do that; my goal with my children is to say what they need to hear to help them grow and help them out of the current drama they've found themselves in, not to punk them.

I'd like to encourage you to put that in your spirit as you're preaching; if these were your kids would you say what you're saying differently? Would you adjust the illustration? Would you come at it from a different angle?

One of the great ways we can care for our audience is to showcase empathy and consider more carefully, in advance, who the audience is and what they might be going through. Are they single, married or divorced? Are they young or old, are they wealthy or poor? When we consider their lives before we preach to them, it may not always change what we say, but it will most often change how you say it.

SPIRIT EMPOWERED

When Jesus was officially releasing his disciples into the work of the great commission, His first command was to WAIT.

In many ways, it was an odd statement when there seemed to be such an urgency on the command. And I'd imagine after seeing Jesus now risen from the dead, they all would have been massively excited and ready to tell the world about the Gospel!

But Jesus says wait. And what was He having them wait on? Power! It was the Holy Spirit that they were instructed to go and wait for. There was a gift and a power from on high.

Conduits Of Power

When God has a message to share, He looks for a lightning rod to send it to Earth! I've heard it phrased like this, God's looking for the amen on Earth to his word in Heaven!

You are not the power of God, but you have been given the privilege to be a carrier and a conduit of that power. You and I have been given authority to release it here on Earth.

When Jesus said He came to set the captives free, this was not a passive statement; He came with authority and power to aggressively take back the people He loves from the grip of the enemy. As preachers we have been given the power of the Spirit of God to bring the powerful word of God that brings healing and freedom!

For the kingdom of God is not a matter of talk but of power.
– 1 Corinthians 4:20 (NIV)

KINGDOM MINDED

Many preaching and communication moments are wasted because they are isolated stories and inspirations that have no greater connection to the purposes of advancing the Kingdom of God!

"This, then, is how you should pray: ""Our Father in Heaven, hallowed be your name, your kingdom come, your will be done, on Earth as it is in Heaven.
— Matthew 6:9-10 (NIV)

Advancing the kingdom!

We are here to establish the Kingdom and to be at the forefront of seeing the kingdom expand on Earth, until it fills the whole Earth! We're not just on a nice cruise ship; we have a destination and a mandate on us to fulfill. For several great years I was able to direct a Bible college in the Seattle area, and one of my favorite moments each year was watching the new students go through the Old and New Testament survey courses. It was powerful to watch the lights come on as people were reminded of the big and eternal purpose that God is working out here on earth.

Give them a compelling vision

"Go To Church" isn't a compelling enough vision, yet that's the biggest driving force in a broader church community. And that's how I learned when I was a youth pastor and God got my attention after a particular high school football season had finished. A young man who was on the football team came to a youth service after I hadn't seen him in a while.

I was excited to see Him and after the basic small talk, I asked how he had been and why I hadn't seen him in a while. He then let me know that he had joined the football team, and the coach told him that to be on that team was going to require everyone on the team to be all in and make the sacrifices needed to change schedule to prioritize the practices and games. At first I was angry about his lack of commitment to coming to church, but then I felt the Holy Spirit challenge me. He said, "That coach gave the young man a more compelling vision as a football coach than I had given for being a consistent part of the church team."

I think that many of us end up slipping into leading and preaching this way. We're preaching to build attendance rather than to advance the kingdom. And when we focus on advancing the purposes of God we'll see the church grow!

Go to: PREACHINGFORWARD.COM
For more preaching videos, resources & downloads.

SECTION TWO
THE CALLING

CHAPTER 5

THE CALLING OF GOD

So Christ himself gave the apostles, the prophets, the evangelists, the pastors and teachers, to equip his people for works of service, so that the body of Christ may be built up until we all reach unity in the faith and in the knowledge of the Son of God and become mature, attaining to the whole measure of the fullness of Christ.
— Ephesians 4:11-13 (NIV)

In this section of the book, we're going to dive into the call to preach! It's key that we drill down into the verses above and other essential verses on the ministry calling, because our preaching and teaching is a response to this calling. To have maximum effectiveness, you must solidify and clarify your calling.

IT'S A CALLING NOT AN OPPORTUNITY.

While it's always a privilege and every speaking moment is a great opportunity, it's important to know that preaching isn't just an opportunity to climb some ministry ladder or build your platform; preaching is a mandate and calling.

When you're heading towards graduation from high school, you take assessments to determine which occupation that you'd be best suited for. The computer then formulates which careers might fit you best. While this may be a helpful exercise, it's not how we get selected for ministry. So we cannot see ministry like a job and career that we're selecting because of qualifications but as a calling that we're being selected for based on God's delegation and choosing.

It's not a choice; it's a delegation.

When you read the above verses in Ephesians, you see that the key leadership roles within the church are established by Jesus. So, our choice is to obey or disobey; to respond yes in faith or to turn and walk away from the calling of God.

The call to follow Jesus in this ministry of preacher is one of the greatest privileges because we get to carry the heart of God to the people He loves. This is also why it's so key to take the time to be a faithful and accurate communicator of the mysteries of the Gospel, so that we don't misrepresent Christ.

Those who God calls to preach are highly blessed and favored, but don't let that go to your head because we see clearly from scripture that not all those God uses are selected because they are the most qualified but because they were the most willing and submitted to the cause of the Kingdom. If I don't represent him and his message well, no matter how talented I am, He has the right to replace me with someone who will.

NOT MY WILL, BUT HIS!

Going a little farther, he fell with his face to the ground and prayed,
"My Father, if it is possible, may this cup be taken from me.
Yet not as I will, but as you will."
— Matthew 26:39 (NIV)

Is your calling based on convenience or obedience? If we're not intentional, the self-serving culture we live in can creep its way into the church and into our pulpits. And while I am fully convinced that God loves to bless those who give up everything for the gospel, the call to preach and to ministry is a call to serve and sacrifice.

Don't base your calling on what Jesus can do for you, instead, with thankfulness, fully submit to the call of God on your life. Like Jesus, during His most intense moments of sacrifice, He says, "not as I will, but as you will." Jesus is the front runner and set the example for us, when we've been given the massive honor to be a leader in His Kingdom, then we have to lay down our agenda and our kingdom for His.

When God calls you, He then takes the time to be sure you've come to that place of total surrender to His purpose. Similar to David's story. He was called and anointed by the Prophet Samuel, but then went right back to taking care of the sheep. That's where He was shaping, molding and purifying the heart of His servant and friend.

CALLING, SACRIFICE & FAVOR

Whenever I'm talking about the call of God on an individual for ministry, I also want to begin with the weight and sacrifice of the call, but serving God isn't just one painful struggle after another. God is a rewarder and blesser of His people and especially those make great sacrifices to advance His purpose on earth.

Yes, there will be great sacrifice and personal inconvenience, but there will also be great reward and fulfillment. For over 20 years now I've been following the call of God on my life and I'm more excited now than the day I first said yes! When you serve God, He takes care of you.

And everyone who has left houses or brothers or sisters or father or mother or wife or children or fields for my sake will receive a hundred times as much and will inherit eternal life.
— Matthew 19:29 (NIV)

CHAPTER 6

CONFIRMING THE
CALL OF GOD

Like I've mentioned several times, preaching isn't a job or a career path; it's a calling. So, how do we know if we're called to preach? Is there a specific path or way we find this out? It's a great and important question that I'll talk through in this section.

I will add a quick caveat before I get into this, that it would be foolish for me to claim to have an exact science or formula for How God calls and then releases you into that call. Because you see in the Bible everything from a more formal call, like the Prophet pouring the oil over David to Saul getting interrupted at random directly from Heaven. But, there are some guidelines and guardrails that will help you walk in your calling.

MY JOURNEY TOWARDS YES!

Let me walk you through my process of being called into ministry, and then talk out other Biblical ways we engage with God's calling.

I didn't grow up in the home of pastors, but my great grandpa T.J. Jones and grandpa John Jones were both powerful preachers and Bible teachers in England and the USA. While I had that heritage, I didn't grow up with the expectation of being a preacher, but I did grow up in a home where my parents, George and Jackie Deuth, loved Jesus passionately and modeled that for me.

In my preteen years is where I really started seeing a hunger for the presence of God and His word intensify, especially once I was filled with the Holy Spirit around age 12!

It was in that 11-13 range that I started feeling God speaking to my spirit about ministry, but like Samuel in the Bible, I didn't yet know the voice of God, so I didn't realize what was happening until later. I even have a distinct memory of being at a church conference, and while the service was going on, me and a few of my friends were running around the back of the room and I heard the preacher from the stage say, "if you feel called to ministry, come forward to receive prayer." I remember stopping and saying to one of my friends, "I think I maybe should respond to that?" but then just kept running and playing with my friends.

As the young teenage years began, I really started feeling that draw to ministry and tried to be around any pastor or preacher that would come through my church. But, the moment that really solidified the calling was when I was just about to enter youth ministry. There was a youth camp and there was a men's camp that had conflicting schedules. Obviously, I wanted to go to the youth camp, but felt bad that my dad was going to have to go to the men's camp without any of his sons with him, so I decided to be the "noble" son and go.

This proved to be the key next step in my calling. During one of the services, there was a time of worship and ministry, and they had someone there that was a prophet or at least moved prophetically. During that service, he called me out and began to prophecy over me, and prophetically declared and confirmed God's calling on my life to full time ministry, and specifically to the role of the evangelist.

Wow! My heart and spirit leapt as I felt that confirmation inside that I was on the right track in what I was feeling, and now I had the confirmation from Heaven that this was God's will for my life.

Then, when I went back to church in the following week and told my pastors and youth pastors that I got called into ministry; they were all basically surprised I hadn't already known that! They again confirmed and affirmed my call to ministry.

It's been 24+ years now since that calling and it's been an incredible faith filled adventure! And great step by step series of saying yes to what God had next. Now, let's talk through a few key points of how God calls and ultimately matures that call.

HOW DOES GOD CALL US?

So Christ himself gave the apostles, the prophets, the evangelists, the pastors and teachers, to equip his people for works of service, so that the body of Christ may be built up until we all reach unity in the faith and in the knowledge of the Son of God and become mature, attaining to the whole measure of the fullness of Christ.
— Ephesians 4:11-13 (NIV)

Jesus calls, appoints and places us into ministry leadership. There are three main ways that He calls us: First, He uses His written word. Second, He calls us by His Spirit. Thirdly, He speaks to us through the current recognized ministry leaders within the church. (Apostle, Prophet, Evangelist, Teacher, Pastor)

Even though I'm listing these out as separate things, they work in unison to clarify your calling like you can see from the read through of my call into ministry.

By His Word

When I was in those initial seasons of being called into ministry, and even now as I've gone through different seasons of the Holy Spirit shaping and clarifying that call, I would often have the Holy Spirit highlight a scripture that was in line with my calling. It was like the Word of God became a mirror reflecting back at me. As I'd read different passages about Evangelists and Prophets, I would feel the Holy Spirit saying to my spirit, "That's You." Jesus used the scripture the declare and confirm His call.

> *"The Spirit of the Lord is on me, because he has anointed me to proclaim good news to the poor. He has sent me to proclaim freedom for the prisoners and recovery of sight for the blind, to set the oppressed free, to proclaim the year of the Lord's favor."*
> *— Luke 4:18-19 (NIV)*

Just to clarify, I'm not suggesting that there are scriptures that were written as prophetic announcements of you and me being called into ministry, like it was for Jesus. Clearly all of scripture was an announcement of His coming and His Kingdom. But, since His Word is living and active, as you're wrestling with your calling, consume the Word and take note of what resonates with you.

By His Spirit

The beginning of a life of ministry requires the breath of God on it, so when you're called to preach and lead His church, the Holy Spirit will speak to your spirit.

While they were worshiping the Lord and fasting, the Holy Spirit said, "Set apart for me Barnabas and Saul for the work to which I have called them."
— Acts 13:2 (NIV)

You'll notice a draw and pull towards ministry. Some feel that at young age like I did, and some not till later in life. But, if you're called to fully give your life to ministry, there will be a growing focus on it and other things will begin to fade in their pull.

Like I shared in my journey, there was a season of maybe a year or so that I began to feel the Spirit calling me, but it took a while for me to fully understand and confirm that call.

By His Leaders

Sometimes our call into ministry begins with us feeling it first, sometimes it begins as others prophetically see God's call on your life and begin to call it out. In my experience it was a combination of both.

God would often speak to people about who was next for a specific ministry or leadership role and send them to call them into it.

The Lord said to him, "Go back the way you came, and go to the Desert of Damascus. When you get there, anoint Hazael king over Aram. Also, anoint Jehu son of Nimshi king over Israel, and anoint Elisha son of Shaphat from Abel Meholah to succeed you as prophet.
— *1 Kings 19:15-16 (NIV)*

Can you just get called to preach without anyone else being involved? Do you need people's approval? My response to that is both yes and no. It's God who calls, and I don't need to chase approval of people to go after something that the Spirit has instructed me to do. But, while there may have been times in Scripture where someone like Paul was called by God and He began in ministry, there later was a echo from Peter and the other apostles that confirmed and affirmed His call.

The Holy Spirit isn't confused or unclear, so if He's called you, then the other ministry leaders will have an echo in their Spirit about it. There's also just basic wisdom and safety in not just running off into a "calling" that you feel, but the trusted and established church leaders aren't on board with. We don't want any self-proclaimed prophets and church leaders that attempt to step into ministry endorsed only by themselves.

STANDING ON A WORD FROM GOD!

I was talking recently with Marcus Lamb, the founder of the Daystar TV network that has an unbelievable global reach for the Gospel! We were talking about ministry calling and his initial response which I echo, is that for anyone to do anything great for God, it's going to require that you have a word from God to be able to stand on to go the distance. Consider this passage:

> *Timothy, my son, I am giving you this command in keeping with the prophecies once made about you, so that by recalling them you may fight the battle well, 19 holding on to faith and a good conscience, which some have rejected and so have suffered shipwreck with regard to the faith.*
> — *1 Timothy 1:18-19 (NIV)*

I have found this principle that, the Apostle Paul is teaching Timothy, to be so true in my life. It's when I'm going through a difficult season in my calling that I must recall the words from God to fight well and overcome. This is why you don't just decide to be in ministry, you are called into it. You are birthed into from the seed of the Word of God.

There have been many seasons where we had to consider all the words from God that had been spoken to us directly by the Holy Spirit or prophetic words through other people. The word from God is like a weapon in my hand to fight off discouragement and any attack of the enemy on my life.

Don't step into ministry, don't try to preach, don't plant a church, don't attempt to start any ministry without a word from God that you can take your stand on.

WHAT COMES AFTER THE CALL?

When I first felt called to preach at 13, I figured the only reason I wasn't getting asked to preach was because I wasn't 16 years old yet and couldn't drive! Haha! I love that wild faith of my thirteen-year-old self! Then when I was 16 and still not getting asked to preach to the world, I decided it must be because I wasn't 18 yet! And then, somewhere in the 16-18-year-old version of me, God began to mature me to understanding that I was going to need preparation and training to fully step into my calling.

So, what comes next after your call into ministry? What do you do after you feel called to preach? That's an important question and later in the book I'm going to share the 7 tests every preacher goes through, but initially let me just remind you that after your BIG call to ministry comes a hidden and obscure season of preparation.

Usually, when we're walking through this season of being hidden, we feel like it's either punishment by God, or it's some person who's trying to hold us back in our calling because of jealousy... however, more likely it's the normal and common process of obscurity that God uses to develop us and prepare us for the calling. Hidden seasons are not God's punishment; they are his protection.

I'm writing a whole book on this concept of how God uses seasons of obscurity, but a general guiding principle to consider is this: if God is the one who promotes and lifts up, then any delays I'm experiencing in my calling must be by his design or He's using it for greater glory. This is so important, because we can too quickly jump to blaming others for our struggles or the delays of the calling of God, but being reminded that nothing on Earth can stop his plan from coming to pass gives me peace and confidence to trust the journey to the all-powerful and wise hand of God.

And when I speak of delay or hidden, I don't mean inactive. As soon as you're called, you can begin to step in that direction, but that beginning development process will often be much longer than anticipated. Also, as a note for those of us who have been in ministry for a while, I've found that God does multiple rounds of this hidden season at new levels. So if you feel a hidden or stalled season again, don't worry, trust that God is shaping something fresh in you.

Humble yourselves, therefore, under God's mighty hand, that
he may lift you up in due time.
— 1 Peter 5:6 (NIV)

STEP INTO YOUR CALLING!

As a final note about your initial calling and confirmation of the call, I want to challenge you to stop second guessing your calling and step into it! If God has called you, and you have an echo of yes from the Church leaders, then stop going back and forth and just begin. And when I say begin, I mean step in that direction. You won't step into all that God has called you to out of the gate, but you start serving and orientating your life in that direction.

And for some of you, you're already past questioning your initial call, but you're not sure if you can pull the trigger and step into a new season of ministry that you feel God speaking to you about it. I've been there before, I found myself stalling out because I wasn't obeying what I knew The Holy Spirit was calling me into. It took a "chance" meeting with a pastor from another part of the nation to bring a prophetic word about direction and to look me in the face and say, just step up and do it!

Let's be in the habit of hearing from God, and immediately obeying. Easier said than done, but while I want to be sure that I'm taking the time to confirm and reaffirm what God is speaking to me, I can start moving into disobedience if I keep asking God for "one more sign" from Him.

If you have a Word from God, that's enough!

43

CHAPTER 7

MATURING AND CLARIFYING YOUR CALLING

When I first felt called to preach, it was a general call to ministry and to the office of the evangelist. In the initial seasons of my calling, I didn't need more than that from God. I wouldn't have known what to do if the Holy Spirit had given me the 20 year plan. But as I obediently and faithfully followed the call, God began to clarify.

Fulfilling your calling is going to be a series of a lot of small steps of obedience. I never anticipated what and how God would orchestrate my steps; I just knew I needed to be faithful with the next step and go from there.

When we start in ministry, most of us would be considered a jack of all trades, or at least we need to see ourselves that way. Learn to jump into a local church and do whatever you can to build and advance the Kingdom of God in that city. Most people's calling doesn't look like a clear straight line; I know mine hasn't. Most of the time, it's jumping from one door of opportunity that God opens to the next one.

Faithfulness and fruitfulness are what open each new door.

I'd say it was about 15+ years into following the call of God that He began to call me to drill in and clarify my primary focus within the ministry calling. While there are many different callings and gifts of the Spirit, there are five specific church leadership roles or gifts within the body of Christ that He gave:

So Christ himself gave the apostles, the prophets, the evangelists, the pastors and teachers, to equip his people for works of service, so that the body of Christ may be built up until we all reach unity in the faith and in the knowledge of the Son of God and become mature, attaining to the whole measure of the fullness of Christ.
— Ephesians 4:11-13 (NIV)

My initial call into ministry was to the role of the evangelist. But it wasn't until the last decade that I've really been operating in that. Along the way, the Holy Spirit began to clarify and speak to me and others about the office of the prophet calling on my life as well. So, when I look at the 5 primary church leadership gifting's I'd say I'm a combination of the evangelist and prophet. As a quick note of clarity, when I use the term "office," I'm referring to someone operating in one of those 5 primary leadership and visionary roles in the church. There's a difference between the role or office of the evangelist and someone who shares their faith, or the office of the pastor and someone who provides spiritual wisdom. As believers, we're all given spiritual gifts as articulated in 1 Corinthians 12, but not all have been called to step into the role of the 5 Ministry Gifts.

There are many that have attempted to help clarify what the primary functions of the 5 Ministry gifts are. As I drilled into them in an attempt to clarify my own calling, this was how I felt like I could best get a handle on the gifts. It's by using the visual and terminology of THE PATH.

If the 5 Ministry roles are designed to lead and mature the church along the PATH, then this is how I see each of their primary functions. This may help you in being able to quickly get a general sense of which one or two you primarily lean towards.

The Apostle: Clears & Reveals The Path
The Prophet: Calls People Back to The Path
The Evangelist: Brings new people onto The Path
The Pastor: Walks with people on The Path
The Teacher: Shows people how to walk on The Path

You may know right away which of the 5 you lean towards, or it may come as you walk out your calling. I find there's usually an initial journey of preparation that God first takes us on to shape our character, and then He clarifies our calling. We all operate in each gift at some level, but we'll tend to lean heavily towards one or two. I'd also like to mention that before you go claiming one of these 5, allow there to be confirmation from the Holy Spirit and from the trusted pastors and ministry leaders around you. Each new season of ministry my wife and I have stepped into was by the prophetic release into the next season of ministry through the pastors and authority that God had positioned us with. Don't step beyond His hand!

OUR FIRST CALL

I want to keep saying and resaying this throughout the book that, as a preacher, my first priority and calling isn't to do the work of ministry but to be with the one who calls us! Jesus is to be the focus of my heart and to have the primary attention of my life. Often we begin in our calling out of passion for His presence, but too quickly move into going through the motions of ministry.

Maybe as you're reading this book, you're at the beginning of your calling and full of passion for Jesus and his presence?! Or, you're someone in ministry who has been serving God's call for years and are going through one of those dry seasons where you look up and realize you've been going through the motions. I know I've had many of those over the course of decades of following the call and each time the Spirit of God lovingly calls me back to His heart!

You have persevered and have endured hardships for my name, and have not grown weary. Yet I hold this against you: You have forsaken the love you had at first. Consider how far you have fallen! Repent and do the things you did at first. If you do not repent, I will come to you and remove your lampstand from its place.
— Revelation 2:3-5 (NIV)

CHAPTER 8

NOTE FOR ITINERATE MINISTRY

Since the beginning of my calling, I sensed God's hand on my life to serve in my local church and to also be sent out to serve and build the broader body of Christ through a variety of ministry. It was about 10+ years of ministry before I really began to travel and minister in churches beyond my own. And at the time of writing this book, it's only been about 4 years since I more fully activated this evangelist and prophet calling. It's often referred to as itinerate or traveling ministry.

But, as we see in scripture and in current history, God calls some of the 5 Leadership roles to travel and serve in capacities beyond their own city. So, I'll have to write more extensively on this after I walk it out more, but let me encourage those who also feel a sense of call to travel and encourage the broader church body.

Go If You're Called

I've already been speaking to this in general, but traveling isn't just something you should try to do because it sounds fun or as a means to try and make extra money.

While itinerate ministry isn't church planting, it does hold some of the same intensity of carving out a new work from nothing like a church plant, which requires travel to be a calling and not a side-gig.

Serve The Church

When I was younger, I heard an evangelist say to a local pastor that he was here to blow in, blow up, and blow out and leave the pastor to clean up the mess. It sounded funny in the moment and got a laugh from the audience, but it's a horribly destructive way to approach your role when you travel. You need to see yourself as serving those God is sending you to.

Give them yourself

Often times we can fall into the trap of feeling like we need to travel and impress the church we're going to so that we get social shout outs, rather than making sure we come to serve and help that pastor mature and move the congregation forward.

Find Your Part to Play

When I was first thinking of itinerating, I knew that I was to serve the church, but I was still too focused on how to fill up my preaching schedule. Along the way, I realized that I needed to figure out my role in building the church, and supporting the incredible pastors who are leading them.

When I was wrestling with this tension, God gave me the idea of the Following Jesus book. After writing and releasing that book, The Holy Spirit really breathed on that and now hundreds of churches around the world in many languages are weekly putting the book to work in making disciples! We've seen over 200k books get into the hands of new believers! And through the impact of that book God began to deepen my heart and passion for helping churches make disciples.

Now, when I travel, it's as much about preaching and ministry as it is about helping support the church I'm with in their discipleship and assimilation strategy. We also created a discipleship and assimilation e-course that you can get at preachingforward.com.

Work With The Pastor

I'd hope this goes without saying, but I've seen too often both while growing up and in current history, evangelists and prophets going rogue and not honoring the hard work that pastors are doing on the ground. Your role as an itinerate isn't to blow in and blow up; it's to come along side that pastor, and with the Holy Spirit, discern how to play a part in moving the church forward!

Go to: PREACHINGFORWARD.COM
For more preaching videos, resources & downloads.

SECTION THREE
CHARACTER

CHAPTER 9

THE CALL TO CHARACTER

Not many of you should become teachers, my fellow believers, because you know that we who teach will be judged more strictly.
— James 3:1 (NIV)

I cannot write on the topic of preaching without taking time to talk about the life of the preacher. I feel like most of my growth as a preacher over the years has been parallel to my personal world growing and strengthening than it was from a new tip or trick in better communication I learned.

It's important for all of us to accept the additional testing and evaluation that the Holy Spirit brings to the life of anyone given the privilege of preaching and ministering God's Word. We won't be sinless as preachers, and we shouldn't try to pretend like we are, but we need to fully embrace that, if we accept the call to preach, then we must embrace God's process of shaping our character.

WHY DOES CHARACTER MATTER SO MUCH?

Of course, we're called to live a life that follows and obeys God's Word, so we want to be in alignment with his commands, but I want to draw our attention to another aspect of this call to strengthen the character and accountability of the preacher.

The first reason why character is so essential is that God cares more about you than He cares about what you do for him. This isn't rocket science, but it is often something we overlook in the pursuit of our calling. When I consider my two beautiful daughters and observe their gifting even at a young age, I get excited with anticipation of all that God can and will do through their lives! But, if there's any area of their lives that seems off centered and inconsistent with sound character, then I'm going to focus my attention on helping them get that part of their lives squared away before pushing them to pursue using their gifts. Why? Because I'm a father who cares about them being healthy and going the distance in life.

God is the same way with us; He doesn't want to use your life at the expense of losing your life as a casualty along the way. So, when He's taking extra time to develop any area of your life and a part of your character, know that He's doing that as a loving father. He's not holding you back; He's actually working on you so that you can go further than you even think possible.

Secondly, the reason why character development of the preacher takes center stage to God is that He is The Good Shepherd, and He's not going to leave His sheep/people to be mismanaged by reckless leaders.

Thirdly, character matters for those of us who preach, because the fall out is greater when a spiritual leader gets off track in sin or other forms of spiritual malpractice. Like many have stated, the higher a contractor wants to build a building, the deeper it's foundations and support structures need to be. The greater the role of influence that God calls you to have, the more shaping and strengthening He's going to do on your character before He releases you! So don't quit on God's process.

CHARACTER IS POWER AND PROTECTION

As The Holy Spirit shapes your character you'll find that it serves you in a couple key ways; it provides you power and protection.

We need a strong resolute conviction of character to boldly speak the truth in a culture of moral relativity. We know that ultimately it's the truth that will set people free. But, initially people rarely want to hear the truth and even reject it and those who carry it. God is looking for bold conduits of his message no matter the social and cultural cost. The only way you and I are going to keep preaching truth is if we're empowered by a character rooted in the truth of God's Word.

A Godly character protects and guards my life. It protects me first and foremost from being polluted by the worldly cultures around me. *We must invade the heart of culture with the Gospel, but not let culture invade the heart of the Gospel.*

THE MESSAGE IS CARRIED ON THE BACK OF YOUR CHARACTER.

There's a weird thing that some preachers will pray or throw into a message because maybe it sounds humble or spiritual but it's not. Maybe you've said or heard somethings like: "God uses me despite me not because of me." Or "Lord, help me get out of the way." While I can certainly see why some may feel the need to make these kinds of statements, I think we're missing that God isn't using humans to carry His message reluctantly or because some better plan fell through; He boldly calls us to partner with him in the ministry of reconciliation. I love this passage where we see the Apostle Paul speaking to this:

so we cared for you. Because we loved you so much, we were delighted to share with you not only the Gospel of God but our lives as well.
— 1 Thessalonians 2:8 (NIV)

If you're preaching to any individual or group of people be encouraged that you, yes you, all of you is the exact packaging that God wanted to use to deliver His message.

With that being said, it's all the more reason why we must allow God to shape and deepen our integrity and character, because when we teach, we're not just repeating a script, we're really giving them ourselves.

The message I preach must be in alignment with the life I live.

Take time to read through the passage below and ask the Holy Spirit to speak to you and highlight any area of your life and character that aren't in alignment with His Word.

Here is a trustworthy saying: Whoever aspires to be an overseer desires a noble task. Now the overseer is to be above reproach, faithful to his wife, temperate, self-controlled, respectable, hospitable, able to teach, not given to drunkenness, not violent but gentle, not quarrelsome, not a lover of money. He must manage his own family well and see that his children obey him, and he must do so in a manner worthy of full[a] respect. (If anyone does not know how to manage his own family, how can he take care of God's church?) He must not be a recent convert, or he may become conceited and fall under the same judgment as the devil. He must also have a good reputation with outsiders, so that he will not fall into disgrace and into the devil's trap.
— 1 Timothy 3:1-7 (NIV)

CHAPTER 10

7 CHARACTER TESTS ALL PREACHERS MUST PASS!

Here are seven key tests that you'll face; embrace each test as a friend, not an enemy. Many of these tests will be uncomfortable and all of them will happen at some level at each new season that God calls you into. There's no shortcut to character development; most of the time, after you're called into ministry, there's a hidden wilderness season of obscurity that God will use to shape your life.

OBEDIENCE TEST

The first test all of us have to pass is the test of obedience. Will you and I be willing to say yes to the call of God and follow him in this role of ministry? Will you be willing to lay down your life and sacrifice it all if needed to follow Jesus and establish His kingdom on Earth? In each and every generation God is looking for someone to step up and answer the call to bring His message to the Earth.

I looked for someone among them who would build up the wall and

stand before me in the gap on behalf of the land so
I would not have to destroy it, but I found no one.
— Ezekiel 22:30 (NIV)

Because of what Jesus has done for us, how can we not respond wholeheartedly if He's called us. And truthfully, I don't see the call to ministry as an option for those who He calls. There's no ability to just "pass" on the call. If He's called you than YES is the only obedient response!

Jonah was one of the most iconic examples of what not to do with the call to preach. He ran the opposite way! That didn't end well for him and, ultimately, it says that the Word of God came to him a second time. So, if you're reading this and feel like you've been running from the call or you delayed the call, don't get depressed about it; simply repent and get back to following and fulfilling this call.

AGENDA TEST

Am I building my kingdom or God's? Most of us begin in ministry out of a passion for people or a heart to know and serve God, and to bring the Good News to the world. If we're not careful in our modern culture, there's such a pull towards fame and popularity, that we can get this all confused in ministry. Since there is public recognition, and since the rise of social media, we can all now see first-hand which preacher is more popular or more followed. This can cause me to build my name and my own fame rather than the name of Jesus.

PEOPLE TEST

Is loving people the focus of your ministry calling, or are people the stepping stones towards your calling? Of course, this is a loaded question and an easy one to quickly answer, but this is a massive deal to Jesus and He really wants to know do you love His people and will you lay down your life for them?

Will you serve and love people or use people? Notice the difference between the way Jesus sees people and the way that the religious leaders of his day saw people:

When the Jews saw the crowds, they were filled with jealousy. They began to contradict what Paul was saying and heaped abuse on him.
— Acts 13:45

When He saw the crowds, He had compassion on them, because they were harassed and helpless, like sheep without a shepherd.
— Matthew 9:36

The religious leaders of that day saw the crowds as a means for validation, power, and influence, among other things, but Jesus saw the crowd as a father who loves his children. This is the way we need to see people so that we care for and love them the way Jesus the good shepherd, wants us to. We must remember that anyone that we've been given the trust to preach to is a privilege, and we must understand that we give an account to God for how we lead His people.

CONGRUENCY TEST

Is my life consistent with the message I preach? We're hitting this topic hard in this whole chapter but wanted to note it here because of its significance. I honestly cannot stress enough the importance of allowing God to dig deep into your life and shine that wonderful and often uncomfortable, light of truth.

No one wants their issues exposed and brought out into the light, but, for your sake and the health of those you preach to, God must take ALL THE TIME He needs to get us ready to carry the message. If there's an area of your life that is in sin and direct disobedience to God, don't give it another moment of permission. Confess it to mentors and friends in your world so that healing and refreshing can come.

You don't have to be perfect to be in ministry but you do have to be honest and transparent and keep engaging areas of weakness so that they don't take you out of your calling.

COURAGE TEST

Am I willing to speak truth when it's not popular and willing to extend grace when it's undeserved.

Not every preacher is going to be elevated to a city, national or global spotlight where you'll have to publically profess a truth you know the world won't like, but some of you will. And all of us at some level will have to deal with the courage test as we're called on to bring God's Word to people. We have to know in advance that it's our job to faithfully bring God's Word to God's people and not just say what people want to hear.

For the time will come when people will not put up with sound doctrine. Instead, to suit their own desires, they will gather around them a great number of teachers to say what their itching ears want to hear.
— 2 Timothy 4:3 (NIV)

STEWARDSHIP TEST

Am I utilizing and developing the gift I've been given? We have a responsibility to steward the call of God well.

Our stewardship will determine our effectiveness and longevity in our calling. It's one thing to know you're called and to say yes to that call, it's another thing to intentionally keep developing that gift to maximize its effectiveness and reach of the Gospel.

If I'm not stewarding my gift or people well, then I will limit and put a cap on my calling. If you've been called to preach to the nations but can't be faithful with a few sheep, then you'll not be promoted.

FIRST LOVE TEST

Do I love God more than my gift? Do I love him first before the praise of men? The praise of men has an intoxicating element to it, but we can also lose the loving feeling for God if we get familiar with his presence or forget His grace, which can get us off track:

I know your deeds, your hard work and your perseverance. I know that you cannot tolerate wicked people, that you have tested those who claim to be apostles but are not, and have found them false. You have persevered

and have endured hardships for my name, and have not grown weary. Yet I hold this against you: You have forsaken the love you had at first. Consider how far you have fallen! Repent and do the things you did at first. If you do not repent, I will come to you and remove your lampstand from its place.
— Revelation 2:2-5 (NIV)

This test is what our calling really flows from; if we lose our first love then we'll lose our way in ministry. Before we go after our calling we must first find our fulfillment in Jesus.

CHAPTER 11

WHAT TO DO WHEN YOUR CHARACTER CRACKS

I don't want to finish this section without first highlighting an important reality; we're all humans and prone to sin and failure. While I personally want to feel the healthy weight and expectation to live above reproach as a preacher, we have to deal with the reality of what to do when the character cracks and fails? Do we quit? Are we done with ministry?

It's easy for us to talk about this topic in a third party type of way as if we don't have character flaws but others might need this section. So, how do we keep ourselves from being another statistic of moral or other character failures in ministry? Because the enemy wants to take you out, knowing that if he can take down the leading man or woman, then he'll create greater destruction to the Kingdom of God.

Keeping our character strong begins with choosing to live in an open and transparent way. It's important to reject the notion that because you're a leader, and specifically a ministry leader, that you cannot be honest and transparent about your temptations and failings. Certainly, there are church environments where you're seemingly not allowed to expose your weaknesses for fear of getting fired, but, if you're in that space, then commit to search out and find a healthy and authentic community. If you're the lead pastor, then create it.

Part of the reason why many pastors fall into sin is because we build a false narrative that we must "have it all together" to be a pastor, which then causes us to hide our issues rather than dealing with them. So, yes, we have to deal with the potential damages and fallout from our sin as a leader, but it's far better to live with integrity before God and people than attempting to keep up a false perception of perfection.

SHINE A LIGHT ON SIN

One of the things I learned to do was to quickly shine light on any areas where my life and character is weak so that I don't end up seeing my life crumble. As a man, like many men, I have to deal with my own lusts and tempting desires that if left unchecked could take me out. And over the years of life before and during ministry, I've had seasons where I was really strong and seasons where I'd give into those temptations. Usually due to late night clicking on social media, where we're all only a few clicks from sin.

For some of you, it might be shocking that I would even put that in this book, but we can't pretend we don't struggle with temptation in different areas. I made it a point to connect with my pastor right away to just say, hey, this is the area of my life that will take me out if anything would. What I find that does is when I expose to the light my areas of sin and weakness, it takes away so much of the power of that sin in my life. It's been a while now since I've given way to any of those sins, but it's not because temptations aren't there, it's because I work hard to deal with sin in its infancy rather than having to face it as a monster later on in life.

Character breakdowns aren't always just in the area of sexual temptation, obviously, there areas of integrity, finances, management of people, and obedience to what God has said and many more.

The first thing we all must do when our character cracks is to come to God first in repentance to receive forgiveness, but then we must confess to our overseers and circle of trusted friendships that can help us walk out healing and restoration.

Therefore confess your sins to each other and pray for each other so that you may be healed. The prayer of a righteous person is powerful and effective.
— James 5:16 (NIV)

Go to: PREACHINGFORWARD.COM
For more preaching videos, resources & downloads.

SECTION FOUR
THE CRAFT

CHAPTER 12

THE CRAFT OF PREACHING

Preach the word; be prepared in season and out of season; correct, rebuke and encourage—with great patience and careful instruction.
— 2 Timothy 4:2 (NIV)

I'm calling preaching a craft, because I want you to think of preaching and teaching, not as some emotionally thrown together concept, but rather a well-crafted work of art taken from the master and delivered with great care to the audience.

The great leadership coach and pastor, John Maxwell, wrote an incredible book on connecting in our communication. He reminds us that our goal in preaching isn't just delivering information, but our goal is to intentionally develop a message that when released, will connect with the listener and help them know and Follow Jesus more fully. We want our messages to land; we want our talks to leave an impact, not so you and I can be remembered, but so Jesus and his word can be known and followed.

Great preaching and communication doesn't come automatically. I wish it did. When I think of the messages that I first preached as a junior high pastor, I start feeling bad for those students! I think, if we're not careful, there can be a subtle assumption that, if God gives me a word to preach, that I'm automatically going to preach amazingly. But, I've found that preaching is like everything that God gives us; it's in seed form. God gives us our gifts, but a part of the journey that we're on is to learn to unpack the gift, to shape it, to submit it back to God and learn to operate it at maximum capacity!

I find that God gives me the words to say, but then I have to give myself to the craft of preaching. This is so much more than just speaking words, it's the process of taking God's Word and planting it into the human heart so that it can produce the fruit it was designed to produce.

OUR RESPONSIBILITY

What are we responsible for as the preacher? First, we're responsible to God to correctly deliver God's Word in its full and undeluded truth. Secondly, we're responsible to the listener to bring the truth to them in a way they can receive it and put it to work. We are not responsible for people rejecting the truth, but we are responsible if people have never heard it.

Now, with that said, many preachers over the years have used that concept as an excuse to be sloppy in their communication. It's true that, at the end of the day, I'm not responsible for your rejection of the truth, but I need to ask myself, "Did I deliver the message of truth and grace well enough so they had a fighting chance of grabbing a hold of it.

That's why it's a craft. It's something to be worked on and labored over. You might think that some are just naturally gifted preachers, but every person you think is a "natural" preacher is someone who labors over that word.

CHAPTER 13

THE MESSAGE

The first aspect of the craft of preaching is the Message itself. I want to highlight a few key parts of every message that you'll want to consider. Before we get into some of these ideas on message development and delivery, I also want you to understand that these are general guiding principles to get you started, but the truth is that each of us has to go on our own journey of discovering our personal style and voice as a communicator.

That process took me a little over ten years of communicating before I really felt like I started to land on my style and feel, so don't rush too quickly into "trying to be yourself." Initially, focus on learning and gleaning from others who preach and teach in a similar way to how you feel most connected with.

HOW TO GET YOUR MESSAGE

This is a common question and the most important since it all begins here. There are really two main ways that you find the message that you're going to preach, and that's within your time with Jesus and with people.

Time with Jesus

Years ago I was doing some training with a group of youth pastors and they asked how I was able to keep getting a message to preach each week. Honestly, the question seemed funny at best but honestly a little concerning that they'd even ask that question because it seemed too basic. The messages we preach always originate in HIM, so the greatest and first place that I go when trying to figure out what I'm going to preach to any group is from my time with Jesus. And that time with God comes in prayer, Bible reading and worship. I hear from God when I lean in and ask the Holy Spirit to speak to me.

There's a passage that God used to challenge me years ago on the importance of taking the time to ask God what He wants me to say to his church:

But if they had stood in my council, they would have proclaimed my words to my people and would have turned them from their evil ways and from their evil deeds.
— Jeremiah 23:22 (NIV)

I wonder how many messages that I just preached a "good" word, but it wasn't the word that my specific audience needed to hear? I never want to preach without taking the time to pause and see if Jesus prompts me on something specific for that upcoming service or class.

While I'll always begin my message preparation with a time of prayer to see if God has something specific to speak, most of the time, I've found that my messages primarily come out of my daily devotional time with God's Word. I have an annual Bible reading plan that I created called, Following Jesus One Year Bible Reading Plan, on YouVersion. Every day it reads sections of the Old Testament, a Psalm/Proverbs and section in the New

Testament. It's been my consistent daily intake of God's Word for years. Each day as I'm reading the word I get 1-3 seed thoughts for a potential message. So then when I'm preparing to preach I'll often start by looking at my daily devotions from that week to see if anything God spoke to me that week is what He's wanting me to bring that weekend.

Remember when God directed His people in the wilderness, that they should only collect mana for that day and then get fresh mana the next day; that's how we need to approach preaching. Go to God daily for a fresh Word from God, first for yourself and then for the people He's called you to preach to.

Time with People

One of the things you notice with Jesus' teaching and many of the Bible writers is they would often teach what that audience was really dealing with in that exact moment.

Some feel nervous about this because they feel like they should just "stick to the text" and preach the word, but you have to ask, why do we preach the word? Why did the Apostle Paul write his letters to the churches? He wrote to disciple them and he wrote to speak to specific things they were dealing with. Never feel bad about building your message from being with people and observing some of their key areas of dysfunction that need to be worked on.

This also ensures that we don't get too far from and out of touch with people. When was the last time you were with unsaved people? When was the last time you were with people from your church or youth ministry to simply hear what situations they're actually facing?

4 CONVICTIONS THAT SHOULD SHAPE YOUR MESSAGE

To help us frame up our approach to developing messages, I want to focus on 4 key areas that we all need to keep in mind as we put a message or teaching together.

Biblically Accurate

I don't think everyone needs to get their doctorate to be able to preach, but everyone who preaches the word must put a massive priority on accurate and true biblical interpretation.

There are many times where I'd be reading a verse, and it jumped out at me in a unique way, and my head gets running down the track of how great this message is going to be and how well people are going to like it. That is, until I begin to dig more into the context of the scripture and find out that I'm not even close to the meaning of the text or that I'm somewhat close, but not fully correct. When that happens, I can either push forward because I know it will preach well, or I can discard that idea and get back to the text. Remember what 2 Timothy says:

> *Do your best to present yourself to God as one approved, a worker who does not need to be ashamed and who correctly handles the word of truth.*
> *— 2 Timothy 2:15 (NIV)*

Some who are reading this come from more of a "stick" to the text kind of a circle and some come from a spirit filled environment like me that asks the Holy Spirit to give us fresh revelation from within the text. I always want to be asking what the Holy Spirit is highlighting and revealing to me, but never let your desire for a "fresh word" get you all caught up in making up things and filling in "gaps" in scripture that God hasn't already filled. Stay true to the text, all fresh revelation from God must fully submit to God's Word! Ultimately, the need for biblical accuracy is about continuing to help people see Jesus in the text.

Here's a great thought from one of my friends on the power of Biblical sound preaching:

One thing that changed everything for me was learning from a few other leaders on "Text-Driven Preaching". This means more than just a desire to preach from the Bible. It is about digging deeper into the original intent of a passage. When we present God's truth more closely to the original intent we can rely on the power of God to carry a message. Something about this relieved the pressure of preaching for me in a significant way. I no longer try to impress. I simply try to be my God-given self, which is an encourager and storyteller while trying to preach the Word with clarity to the original intent and I know the results are not up to me.
They are up to God.
— Matt Brown | Think Eternity

If you are new to preaching and ministry, I'd highly recommend you going to Bible college where you're able to get training on biblical study and interpretation. I am a huge fan of church internship programs, but make sure that internship is partnered with theological training. You need both hands on practical experience and Biblical training. That's why I love the internship at our church, there's a strong emphasis on both.

Help People

When I first began to preach I got this advice from Kevin Gerald, I was told before I got up to speak I should look around the room and say to myself, "I love these people!" This is a simple but powerful way to refocus your mind on serving people rather than on being nervous.

Let your focus on helping people drive the development of your message. The reason why this is so key is that too often preachers are trying to impress people rather than help people. But, Jesus gave the church leadership roles to equip the Church not to impress the Church.

> *Preach the word; be prepared in season and out of season; correct, rebuke and encourage—with great patience and careful instruction.*
> *— 2 Timothy 4:2 (NIV)*

You'll notice that this verse packs a massive punch and gives some great insight into the types of things we should be preaching on that will help mature people.

Another note: stay honest, open and authentic with your audience. We don't help people by pretending to be perfect; we're much more helpful when we allow people to see us authentically living out the principles within the Bible.

Carry Power

Many times people settle for "good" preaching without actual demonstration of God's power. I'm encouraging you to preach the Word, and release its full and undiluted power.

> *My message and my preaching were not with wise and persuasive words, but with a demonstration of the Spirit's power, so that your faith might not rest on human wisdom, but on God's power.*
> *— 1 Corinthians 2:4-5 (NIV)*

This verse should challenge and convict us all! How many times over the years have I settled for "wise" and persuasive talks that didn't move into demonstrating God's power. The Message is what carries the seed, which is the Word of God! The power is in God's Word!

The three main things that cause us to preach without power are poor theology, no example and fear. Many never even think to expect the supernatural when they preach because someone told them that was just in the Bible times. I'm not here to do a complete study on it; all I ask is that you just read the scriptures without "the gifts aren't for today" mindset, and see how The Holy Spirit reveals his desire to partner in power with the preaching of the Word! Many would theologically believe that God's power is available to us today but have never seen it done in a healthy way or even modeled at all.

My encouragement is to reach out and find out who is modeling it well. And I'd genuinely say my lead pastors, Jurgen and Leanne Matthesius and our global C3 Church movement leaders, pastor Phil and Chris Pringle, are some of the best at modeling power and wisdom in both preaching and the demonstration of the Spirit's Power. And the last and most common thing that shuts down the gifts of the Spirit is fear. Fear of not doing it "right" or fear of what people might think, but I want to challenge you to step out in faith and activate the gifts the Holy Spirit has given you to build up and strengthen the church.

One of the simplest and most consistent ways you can do this is to lay hands on people who need prayer for healing, wisdom or breakthrough of some kind. As you take the step of faith to invite people to respond and lay hands on them, you'll find that the power of God will meet you in those moments to heal, guide, and give you prophetic words that they need for that moment.

And it all begins with breathing faith into the atmosphere as you call people to trust and believe God.

One of our primary roles as preachers is to release faith!
– Jurgen Matthesius

Call People To Action!

Where is your message leading people? It's not good enough for people to just listen to God's Word, it's key that they act upon it to begin to see the transformation happen in their lives. So, it stands to reason that when you preach God's Word there should always be a call to action. There should be something that calls them to act on what they just heard. Our goal as preachers is not just to inform people but to call people forward.

In the same way, faith by itself, if it is not accompanied by action, is dead.
— James 2:17 (NIV)

CHAPTER 14

HOW TO WRITE
YOUR MESSAGE

I'm going to talk you through my message writing process, and for quick reference you can go to preachingforward.com and download my one-page Message Writing Check-list. Now, let's talk through my five step process for writing a message.

1. CHOOSE A SCRIPTURE OR TOPIC

I detailed this out in more length in the beginning of this chapter, so I'll just note for quick reference, the main ways that I get my message topics are from daily Bible reading, seeking direction from the Holy Spirit, and observing culture.

The other key ways are from observing the needs of the audience I'm about to speak to and direction from the church that I'm preaching at. While both of those sound less spiritual, they are still important and powerful ways to decide what to preach. Consider some of the parables that Jesus taught, they were a response to the needs of the people He was teaching. Also, most of the content of the apostle Paul's letters were a response to the needs and issues that those churches were facing.

If you think of it like parenting; each day I don't ask the Holy Spirit what exactly He wants me to teach my kids today. Most of the time, my teaching is a response to my observation of their attitudes and behaviors. Now, yes, I do pray for my kids and ask God for wisdom and guidance in parenting them, and I use scripture to consider how I need to be loving and leading them.

Having said that, I'd say that a local pastor may lean more towards considering more of a healthy balanced diet of messages and topics where the itinerate preacher would tend to lean more into receiving a fresh word from God for that specific service. Both callings should lean into what God is saying and also what the people need.

2. UNLOAD YOUR SPIRIT AND MIND

This step may vary in length depending on your own personal experience and knowledge of the topic. In this step after I identify the direction that I want to go, I get a notebook out or my laptop/phone and begin to jot down as many key thoughts that come to mind on that topic and things like illustrations, personal experiences and other things like that. The reason why I'd encourage you to begin with this step before you start doing any research is that sometimes this process and space is where the Holy Spirit can bring to your mind or stir things up that are already in you. If the topic of your message was something that came to your spirit, often there are some other things the Holy Spirit will want to bring to you. So, pause and first begin to get it all out on paper. No thought or verse or illustration should be left off the table in this moment. Even if you don't think it will be good, start by doing that, and then we can shape the message in further steps.

3. RESEARCH & STUDY

Once you've unloaded what's already in you, it's time to diligently research the topic and study the scriptures. Don't just settle for what you already know; do the work of unearthing the gold in the Word of God on that specific topic, and discover what in culture can help you connect God's Word effectively with your audience.

Here's a quick list of the kinds of things to research that will enhance your messages:

- Scripture references
- How is current culture handling this topic
- Illustrations or stories
- Statistics
- Personal life example
- Quotes
- Is there a physical prop that will really clarify this message?
- Humor: find a funny story or write your own
- Lyrics to a song
- Excerpt from a book
- Imagine if…
- Draw on the power of their imagination
- Modern day parables
- Movie reference/clip

However, this step is more than just researching for cool ideas and illustrations, this is the part where you really study out scripture to make sure that every message you have is rock solid theologically.

I'm so passionate about Biblical accuracy. I don't care how great is sounds or how well it rhymes; if it's not firmly grounded in God's Word, then don't preach it. Some theological themes in scripture don't have to be re-clarified each time you preach, but before you take on a new area of scripture that you haven't touched yet, make sure you dig in until you get clarity, or as clear as possible. I use a lot of online study tools now and a few phone apps that allow me to do a deeper study of the original languages, which reveals richer meaning and context to the story. I also do some study by simply cross-referencing the translations of the Bible during study. My primary translation, where I do my daily Bible reading and my preaching from, is the NIV. But, when I'm studying, I use a combination of NIV, a paraphrases like The Message, and the Amplified translation, which basically allows you to do quick word studies as you study.

I do want to highly encourage anyone who is called to preach to take time and invest in getting Biblical theology training. Getting Systematic theology instruction will save you and your audience a ton of heartache from miss interpretation of scripture. Not every preacher needs to get a doctoral degree, but two to four years of training should be minimum. And I think Bible college training partnered with practical ministry training is ideal. Our internship at C3 Church, partners both of these well.

4. SHAPE & CLARIFY THE MESSAGE

At this stage of the message development process, you basically have a big mound of concepts, scriptures, illustrations, revelations, quotes and more; and now the real work begins. Honestly, this step is one of the things that separates average communicators from those preachers really making an impact. It's your willingness to work the message through until it takes shape. It's like a clump of raw material that you're beginning the sculpting process to slowly reveal the masterpiece.

When I was first learning to preach, I was mentored and coached by an incredible and powerful preacher, John Morgan, who taught me some of these key disciplines. He would have me print out all of the content from the first few steps and then layout the pages on the table and begin the process of circling, highlighting, deleting and making all kinds of markings to note where I wanted to move content around in the message. After a few minutes of making notes on that copy, I'd go to the computer, make the edits and updates and then print out the pages and repeat the process. Often doing that 10+ times.

There are a few key things I look for when I'm in this message shaping and clarifying process. First, based on where I feel the message is supposed to go, I identifying which thoughts can quickly be eliminated. (Which I keep a separate Word document of the content I delete just incase it ends up finding a good fit later.) As you do that, it begins to more clearly reveal the pictures of the message. This process helps me better clarify the direction or purpose of the message. The clearer you are about the goal of the message in your preparation, the more effective you'll be on the stage.

The other key driving concept that I learned from John that shapes my messages is the maintaining of logical progression of thought. Too often, someone will preach a 3 point message and, as you listen to it, it's good content but there just seems to be a disconnect between each concept and, ultimately, it leaves people stranded. So, I don't want to begin with point 1, then jump to what should be point 3 and then back to 2 and attempt to wrap it up. Logical progression of thought in the message just simply means does each of the elements of the message naturally and logically lead from one point or concept to the next? As you're doing this message shaping and clarifying practice, you'll start being able to better see if each section is building on the last, or if it's jumping around too much for the listener.

Don't settle for the first draft of your message. Be a wise and good steward of the gift that God has given you.

5. PRAY IT HOT!

And last but not least, Pray that message hot! There are many obvious reasons why this is important, but one of the main reasons why this is so crucial for me is that during the study and the shaping process, that once exciting message can get lost as you drill into the fine details of the flow of the message, and we start thinking we're just communicating ideas. However, a time of prayer brings me back to the heart of the matter and allows me to reengage with the original passion to preach that message I had at first.

But if I say, "I will not mention his word or speak anymore in his name," his word is in my heart like a fire, a fire shut up in my bones. I am weary of holding it in; indeed, I cannot.
— Jeremiah 20:9 (NIV)

CHAPTER 15

THE DELIVERY

As we wrap up this book, let's get into some practical notes on preaching. Here are some keys to make sure that we deliver a message or put together a teaching that's effective and powerful.

YOUR FOCUS BEFORE YOU PREACH:

Focus on the people.

In preparation and literally right before you preach, declare, "I love these people." Get your eyes off yourself "doing well," and get your eyes focused on serving the people God has put in front of you.

Focus on knowing your audience.

Before you preach, take the time, as best you can, to understand the world they live in. What are the common battles they're facing that might be unique to them?

Focus on being Effective.

Let your mindset not be on hoping you do well or that they like you, but set your focus on being the most effective you can be at delivering that message.

Focus on what the Holy Spirit is speaking in the moment.

One of the benefits of studying well is that you're able to be more at ease and ready to lean into what the Spirit might want you to adjust or shift in the moment.

WHEN YOU PREACH

Focus on the people not your notes.

The notes should be a general reference point for you but you shouldn't be doing a lot of reading from your notes or you'll create a disconnect with your audience.

Read your audience but don't overly react to them.

It's a good skill to learn how to read and sense from God if you feel like your audience is connecting with the content you're preaching, and if you need to tweak it a bit on the fly to really help them grasp the concept. But the key is that you don't freak out or get reactive purely because someone has a bored or grumpy look on their face. When I was first learning how to preach, my main audience was junior high age students who aren't super visually supportive when you preach, so I learned how to be confident in preaching without getting a lot of audience visual response.

Bring humor to your message.

We all have our own "funny". It's true, in our own ways, we can add humor and help our audience open up to laugh, and then receive what God is trying to do in their lives. But, the key is to find your personal flow of what funny is. I'm not a joke teller, but I do like to comment on the constant humor that is found in our daily lives. Some planned and some in the moment.

Be transparent.

Don't hold back or pretend you got it together. Allow your humanity to show through. Telling stories on yourself and helping people see how you have struggled, wrestled and had victory in your life will be so key in helping people engage with your message.

Be You.

We've already talked about this, but your audience doesn't need you to be another version of any other great preacher. They need you to fully bring yourself to the moment.

Your most comfortable communication style is your most effective communication style. preaching that isn't "authentically you" doesn't carry the specific anointing that God has placed on your life. It's ok to learn from what everyone else is doing but when it comes to the delivery of your

sermon, it must be a reflection of your cadence, your style, your emphasis and your culture. be true to both the WHAT and HOW of your preaching style.
— *Russell Johnson | The Pursuit*

Be Mindful Of Your Cadence.

When preaching or teaching, we can often lean towards being super chill or being at a level 10 passion, but the key is using both ends of the spectrum and everywhere in-between to create a cadence and rhythm to your message that is engaging. The audience tunes out if you're at a constant monotone level 1 or a monotone level 10. Like a great symphony, help people lean into the message by creating crescendos and decrescendos in your pace and volume.

Use Movement Purposefully.

If I'm honest, I can tend to move too much when I preach, but the key is that we're intentional about the movements we make. If you pace fast and non-stop, the audience will get dizzy, but, if you stand still and don't move at all, it could feel robotic and put them to sleep. Use movement to emphasize a point or a moment.

Don't Hide Behind The Pulpit.

The podium or tables we preach and teach from can be so varied, but I just want to make a note not to "hide" behind it. The pulpit can create a subtle and invisible barrier between you and your audience. Only be standing behind the podium to read your notes, but don't live there.

Don't be an echo but rather find your own unique voice
— Benny Perez | The Church LV

WHEN YOU CLOSE THE MESSAGE

Landing The Plane.

Sometimes, if we're not careful, we can put all of our focus in message preparation on how to begin the sermon, and then how to put together the key points, and then leave the end to "wing it." I know I've done that, and it doesn't go well. Sure there are some things I'll feel out in the moment, but it's key that I know in advance how I want to land this message. How are we going to bring a clear next step of faith and action related to what was just said? Always point people to the action step they need to take.

Calling People To Follow Jesus.

For me, my goal, in addition to the specific call to action from the message, is to always give people an opportunity to respond to Jesus. When you call people to that point of decision, be bold about. Don't apologize or use soft-sell language to try and get more people to respond. When you call someone to Christ, you're calling them to lay down their lives, pick up their cross and Follow Jesus. There is nothing light about that and how we call someone to Jesus is usually how they live for Him. Also, unless the message is specifically evangelistic, I usually see the altar call/salvation call as a separate segment. Sometimes I do it right at the end of the message or I'll do it after I give the first response to the message itself.

Calling People To The Altar.

Depending on your church culture, this concept of calling people out of their seats to come forward to the stage might be standard or may be completely foreign to you, but I want to encourage you on the power of this practice. Sometimes, I'll do this when I'm calling people to Follow Jesus, or sometimes it's to receive prayer or spend time with God in response to the message. A few of the massive benefits of doing this is that it engages their faith when they take a physical response to what God is doing. It also elevates their faith and expectation to look to God and receive what He's wanting to do in their lives. Also, it creates a more natural space for you and other church leaders to lay hands on people in prayer. A couple things I've learned with this: if you're confident about calling people forward, they will come. Don't be timid when you call people to respond. Make sure that the worship team is ready to play and join you in setting the atmosphere for people to encounter God.

Activating The Gifts Of The Spirit.

Preaching has the Holy Spirit all over it from start to finish, but what I'm emphasizing here is activating the gifts of the spirit, like prophecy, miracles and others. Obviously, you don't have to wait till you're ending your message to use the gifts of the Spirit, but that is most often when I step into that since the worship and preaching of the word has now softened the hearts of people to be ready to receive from God. I will do more extensive training and writing on this topic, but for this quick section let me say this, learning to powerfully move in the Spirit during ministry is one of the most impacting things we can do as a preacher and teacher. So, if you already know how to minister this way let me encourage you to do it more and more. If it's a new concept, and you're hungry for it, then begin by finding a mentor who is able to help guide and stir you up in the things of the Spirit, as well as embrace the faith step it takes to activate the gifts. My pastor, Jurgen, helped me years back with the simple and practical understanding of how to operate these spiritual weapons we've been given. When asking him about this, he simply said that gifts of the Spirit are activated or operated by faith. This means that, often, you have to step out in faith before the prophetic word is released or before the power for healing comes.

Go to: PREACHINGFORWARD.COM
For more preaching videos, resources & downloads.

FINAL CHALLENGE

I'll leave you with one of the verses that has profoundly shaped my preaching and ministry over the years and I hope gets embedded into your spirit as you write and preach for the years to come.

But if they had stood in my council, they would have proclaimed my words to my people and would have turned them from their evil ways and from their evil deeds.
— Jeremiah 23:22 (NIV)

Every time I read this verse it reminds me of a couple important things. First, that any audience I'm preaching to are His loved people. Second, God knows what his people need to experience transformation. Finally, it shows us the formula to get God's Words to His people; the messenger needs to spend time in God's presence. He designed it this way so that our role as preachers would always keep us close to His heart.

With that in mind, let's focus less on coming up with something to say, and stay committed to delivering what Jesus has already said, so that His people will turn back to the Father.

I'll end with this prayer:

Lord, we love you and we're firstly so thankful to have been called to follow you and receive your grace for salvation! And as if that wasn't enough, you've honored us when the Holy Spirit called us to be preachers, teachers and messengers of your Gospel! Holy Spirit, give us wisdom and prophetic insight to bring the word that your people need and give us the courage to boldly deliver that word!

And Lord, I pray for each reader of this book, that you would bless them for saying yes and answering this call, and I ask that when they accurately, clearly and boldly preach the Word, that you would show up in power and confirm your word with supernatural signs following!

Till our last breath we are committed to fulfilling the great commission that you gave us! We will listen for your words, we will give ourselves diligently to study and we will release your word with the authority you gave us! Let your kingdom come and your will be done here on Earth as it is in Heaven! Amen!

I'm praying this book was an encouragement to you and your calling to preach and to ministry leadership! I'd love to hear from you and connect! Reach out to me via email or any social media.

Talk soon…
Samuel Deuth

All Social: @samueldeuth
Direct: sjd@samueldeuth.com

Preach the word; be prepared in season and out of season; correct, rebuke and encourage—with great patience and careful instruction.
— *2 Timothy 4:2 (NIV)*

ABOUT THE AUTHOR

Samuel is a passionate follower of Jesus, in love with his beautiful wife, Katie, and loves being a father to his two incredible girls, Mercedes and Kenzie. He and his wife are a part of the pastoral team at C3 Church in San Diego, CA and the C3 Americas Regional Operations Directors. They also travel and preach the Gospel around the globe with a passionate and prophetic edge! Their ministry encourages churches through a variety of ministry and training resources.

A couple key resources are their ministry to preachers called, *Preaching Forward*, and their work with pastors and church leaders to help enhance their discipleship effectiveness through his best-selling discipleship book, *Following Jesus*.

To connect with Samuel or Katie, and for speaking and coaching inquiries, contact them on social media or at samueldeuth.com

MORE RESOURCES

Discipleship Resources for your church
followingjesusbook.com

Samuel & Katie Deuth
Videos, Devotionals, Resources, Ministry Coaching
samueldeuth.com

Preaching Resources
preachingforward.com

Made in the USA
Lexington, KY
10 December 2019